PRUDENT PRACTICES FOR INVESTMENT STEWARDS
(U.S. EDITION)

AICPA EDITORIAL STATEMENT TO READERS

The Personal Financial Planning Division of the American Institute of Certified Public Accountants (AICPA) has served as the technical editor for "Prudent Practices for Investment Stewards (U.S. Edition)" (Handbook). The AICPA's participation in the development of the Handbook is intended to promote and protect the interests of the consumer public and to perpetuate the delivery of competent and objective investment advice.

The Handbook was developed specifically for Investment Stewards – trustees, investment committee members, attorneys, accountants, institutional investors, and anyone else who is involved in managing investment decision-making. The Handbook will serve as a foundation for prudent investment fiduciary practices. It provides investment fiduciaries with an organized process for making informed and consistent decisions. Fiduciaries must, however, exercise professional judgment when applying the Practices; consulting legal counsel and other authorities when appropriate.

The investment fiduciary practices contained within this Handbook have not been approved, disapproved, or otherwise acted upon by any senior technical committee of the American Institute of Certified Public Accountants and have no official or authoritative status. The AICPA's participation is solely in the capacity of a technical editor.

Although the fiduciary practices primarily focus on many of the legal requirements of investment fiduciaries, the scope of the Handbook addresses the Employee Retirement Income Securities Act (ERISA), the Uniform Prudent Investor Act (UPIA), and the Uniform Management of Public Employee Retirement Systems Act (MPERS). Investment Stewards must become familiar, and comply, with all other federal and state laws applicable to the fiduciary's particular field of practice including the rules and restrictions imposed by regulatory bodies such as the Securities and Exchange Commission, General Accounting Office, Department of Labor/ERISA and the Internal Revenue Service.

We gratefully acknowledge the invaluable contributions of the many CPA's who were instrumental in the review of the Handbook. The PFP Division would also like to acknowledge the special efforts of Raymond J. Cobos, CPA/PFS, Joel Framson, CPA/PFS, Clark M. Blackman II, CPA/PFS, Paul J. Bracaglia, CPA, AIF®, Ken A. Dodson, CPA/PFS, Charles R. Kowal, JD, CPA, Michele L. Schaff, CPA/PFS, AIFA®, and Scott K. Sprinkle, CPA/PFS.

The AICPA is the national professional organization of CPAs, with more than 330,000 members in business and industry, public practice, government, and education. For more information about the AICPA, visit its Web site at *www.aicpa.org*.

Table of Contents

Prudent Practices for Investment Stewards (U.S. Edition)

PRUDENT PRACTICES FOR INVESTMENT STEWARDS (U.S. EDITION)

INTRODUCTION

PRUDENT PRACTICES FOR INVESTMENT STEWARDS
(U.S. EDITION)

This publication is part of a series of fiduciary handbooks published by Fiduciary360 to define Global Standards of Excellence for investment fiduciaries. The handbooks are designed to be reference guides for knowledgeable investors, as opposed to in-depth "how to" manuals for persons who are not familiar with basic investment management procedures. Handbooks are available through Fiduciary360 (fi360.com) or through any of the Distribution Partners listed on the next page

Handbooks that are referenced as a "U.S. Edition" are fully substantiated by U.S. legislation, case law, and regulatory opinion letters. Handbooks that are referenced as a "Worldwide Edition" are substantiated by industry best practices.

Prudent Practices for Investment Stewards
(U.S. Edition)

Fiduciary practices for persons who have the legal responsibility for managing investment decisions (trustees and investment committee members).

Prudent Practices for Investment Advisers *(U.S. Edition)*

Fiduciary practices for professionals who provide comprehensive and continuous investment advice, including wealth managers, financial advisors, trust officers, investment consultants, financial consultants, financial planners, and fiduciary advisers.

Legal Memoranda *(U.S. Edition)*

Legal opinions and substantiation for all of the practices defined for Investment Stewards and Investment Advisors in the U.S.

Prudent Practices for Investment Stewards and Investment Advisors *(Worldwide Edition)*

Fiduciary practices which define a Global Standard of Excellence for Investment Stewards and Investment Advisors.

Fiduciary360 has also developed handbooks and substantiation for Canada, New Zealand, and Singapore.

Prudent Practices for Investment Managers
(Worldwide Edition)

Fiduciary practices which define a Global Standard of Excellence for Investment Managers – professionals who have discretion to select specific securities for separate accounts, mutual funds, commingled trusts, and unit trusts.

Fiduciary360 is also a founding member of **CEFEX** (Centre for Fiduciary Excellence), which is a global initiative established to define and promote Global Fiduciary Standards of Excellence, and to serve as an independent rating and certification organization.

CEFEX *has chosen the stylized version of the Greek letter "Phi," to represent fiduciary "trustworthiness" and/or "excellence."*

As a certifying organization, **CEFEX** also defines formal procedures to assess whether an investment fiduciary is in conformance with defined practices. An entry level verification is a first-party assessment, referred to as a SAFE™ (Self-Assessment of Fiduciary Excellence). A corresponding SAFE has been created for each handbook in the fiduciary series.

DISTRIBUTION PARTNERS

The following organizations serve as distributors for the fiduciary handbooks and SAFEs.

Alpha Wealth Strategies	www.alphawealthstrategies.com
Ardor Fiduciary Services, Ltd.	www.prudentfiduciary.com
Bruton Financial Advisors, LLC	www.brutonfinancial.com
BST Retirement Services, LLP	www.bstco.com
Charles Stephen & Co., Inc.	www.charlesstephen.com
Chubb Group	www.chubb.com
Comerica, Inc.	www.comerica.com
Commonfund	www.commonfund.org
Cornerstone Advisors Asset Management, Inc.	www.cornerstone-companies.com
Delaware Investments	www.delawareinvestments.com
Deutsche Bank	www.db.com
Federated Investors	www.federatedinvestors.com
Fidelity Investments	www.fidelity.com
Freund & Co. Investment Advisors, L.C.	St. Louis, MO
Gartmore Global Investments	www.gartmore.us
Halbert Hargrove	www.halberthargrove.com
The Broker-Dealers of ING	www.ingadvisors.com
Ingham Group	www.ingham.com
Inspired Capitalworks	www.inspiredcapitalworks.com
Lindner Capital Advisors	www.lcaus.com
Managed Accounts Consulting Group of Prudential Investors	www.managedaccounts.com
Managers Investment Group	www.managersinvest.com
McKinley Investment Group, Inc.	www.mckinleyadvisors.com
Midwest Fiduciary	www.midwestfiduciary.com
National Association of College and University Business Officers (NACUBO)	www.nacubo.org
Plante Moran Financial Advisers	www.pmfa.com
Silver Oak Wealth Advisors, LLC	www.silveroakwa.com
Sprinkle Financial Consultants, LLC	Scott@sprinklefinancial.com
Stanton Group	www.stanton-group.com
Thornburg Investment Management	www.thornburginvestments.com
Victory Asset Management Co., Inc.	www.victoryasset.com
Wealth Management Strategies	www.wealthdirection.com
Wharton Advisors	www.whartonadvisors.net

An investment fiduciary is someone who is managing the assets of another person and stands in a special relationship of trust, confidence, and/or legal responsibility.

IT'S ABOUT PROCESS

The vast majority of the nation's liquid investable wealth is in the hands of investment fiduciaries, and the success or failure of investment fiduciaries can have a material impact on the fiscal health of this country. As critical as their role is, more needs to be done to define the details of a fiduciary's prudent investment process.

This handbook is about the Practices a fiduciary should follow to demonstrate prudence in managing investment decisions. By following a structured process based on these Practices, the fiduciary can be confident that critical components of an investment strategy are being properly implemented.

The term, "fiduciary," can be divided further into three groups:

> **Investment Steward** – *A person who has the legal responsibility for managing investment decisions (including trustees and investment committee members).*

> **Investment Advisor** – *A professional who is responsible for managing comprehensive and continuous investment decisions (including wealth managers, financial advisors, trust officers, financial consultants, investment consultants, financial planners, and fiduciary advisers).*

> **Investment Manager** – *A professional who has discretion to select specific securities for separate accounts, mutual funds, commingled trusts, and unit trusts.*

Editorial Note: This document uses the terms "adviser" and "advisor."

"Adviser," as in "fiduciary adviser," is in reference to the term defined by the 2006 Pension Protection Act.

"Advisor," as used by Fiduciary360 throughout its materials, refers to the professional who is providing comprehensive and continuous investment advice.

Investment Stewards, along with their Investment Advisor if the Steward has retained one, have the most important, yet most misunderstood, role in the investment process: to manage the investment Practices (defined in this handbook), without which the other components of the investment strategy cannot be defined, implemented, or evaluated. The Investment Steward is responsible for **managing** the overall investment strategy: deciding on the asset allocation, defining the details of the strategy, implementing the strategy with appropriate Investment Managers, and monitoring the strategy on an ongoing basis.

IT'S ABOUT EXCELLENCE

This handbook also defines a Global Standard of Excellence and what can be done to improve an Investment Steward's decision-making process. The excellence is established by twenty-two *Practices* which are intended to provide the framework of a disciplined investment process.

The twenty-two *Practices* are organized under a four-step Fiduciary Quality Management System. The steps are consistent with the global ISO 9000 Quality Management System standard, which emphasizes continual improvement to a decision-making process:

Step 1: Organize
(Practices that begin with S-1.__)

Step 2: Formalize
(Practices that begin with S-2.__)

Step 3: Implement
(Practices that begin with S-3.__)

Step 4: Monitor
(Practices that begin with S-4.__)

For each of the twenty-two *Practices*, one or more *Criteria* are provided to establish the scope of the Practice, and to help define the details of the *Global Fiduciary Standard of Excellence*.

The *Practices* represent the minimum process prescribed by law; the *Criteria* represent the details of the Global Standard of Excellence.

Fiduciary Quality Management System

(Consistent with the ISO 9000 QMS Continual Improvement Process)

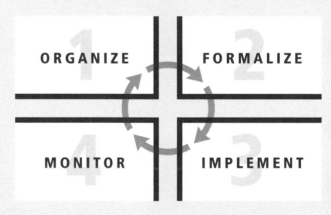

Components of a Standard

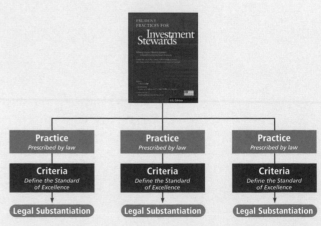

The twenty-two *Practices* for Investment Stewards are a mirror image of the *Practices* that have been defined for Investment Advisors, since the primary role of the Advisor is to assist with the management of the Steward's fiduciary roles and responsibilities.

Investment Managers, on the other hand, have a unique role and an additional twenty-four *Practices* have been defined for evaluating whether an Investment Manager is worthy of a fiduciary mandate.

In total, forty-six different fiduciary *Practices* have been identified, detailing a prudent process for Investment Stewards, Investment Advisors, and Investment Managers. These *Practices* are summarized in "*The Periodic Table of Global Fiduciary Practices*," copied below, but can be viewed in more detail in the foldout in the back of the handbook.

The Periodic Table of Global Fiduciary Practices

Practice M-1.1 Senior management demonstrates expertise in their field, and there is a clear succession plan in place.	**Practice M-1.2** There are clear lines of authority and accountability, and the mission, operations, and resources operate in a coherent manner.			**Practice SA-2.1** An investment time horizon has been identified.	**Practice SA-2.2** A risk level has been identified.	**Practice M-2.1** The organization provides disclosures which demonstrate there are adequate resources to sustain operations.	**Practice M-2.2** The organization has a defined business strategy which supports their competitive positioning.
Practice M-1.3 The organization has the capacity to service its client base.	**Practice M-1.4** Administrative operations are structured to provide accurate and timely support services and are conducted in an independent manner.	**Practice SA-1.1** Investments are managed in accordance with applicable laws, trust documents, and written investment policy statements (IPS).	**Practice SA-1.2** The roles and responsibilities of all involved parties (fiduciaries and non-fiduciaries) are defined, documented, and acknowledged.	**Practice SA-2.3** An expected, modeled return to meet investment objectives has been identified.	**Practice SA-2.4** Selected asset classes are consistent with the identified risk, return, and time horizon.	**Practice M-2.3** There is an effective process for allocating and managing both internal and external resources and vendors.	**Practice M-2.4** There are effective and appropriate external management controls.
Practice M-1.5 Information systems and technology are sufficient to support administration, trading, and risk management needs.	**Practice M-1.6** The organization has developed programs to attract, retain, and motivate key employees.	**Practice SA-1.3** Fiduciaries and parties in interest are not involved in self-dealing.	**Practice SA-1.4** Service agreements and contracts are in writing, and do not contain provisions that conflict with fiduciary standards of care.	**Practice SA-2.5** Selected asset classes are consistent with implementation and monitoring constraints.	**Practice SA-2.6** There is an IPS which contains the detail to define, implement, and manage a specific investment strategy.	**Practice M-2.5** The organization has a defined process to control its flow of funds and asset variation.	**Practice M-2.6** Remuneration of the company and compensation of key decision-makers is aligned with client interests.
	Practice M-1.7 There is a formal structure supporting effective compliance.	**Practice SA-1.5** Assets are within the jurisdiction of courts, and are protected from theft and embezzlement.	**ORGANIZE 1**	**FORMALIZE 2**	**Practice SA-2.7** The IPS defines appropriately structured, socially responsible investment (SRI) strategies (where applicable).	**Practice M-2.7** The organization has responsible and ethical reporting, marketing, and sales practices.	**Practice M-2.8** There is an effective risk-management process to evaluate both the organization's business and investment risk.
Practice M-4.1 There is a defined process for the attribution and reporting of costs, performance, and risk.	**Practice M-4.2** All aspects of the investment system are monitored and are consistent with assigned mandates.	**Practice SA-4.1** Periodic reports compare investment performance against appropriate index, peer group, and IPS objectives.	**MONITOR 4**	**IMPLEMENT 3**	**Practice SA-3.1** The investment strategy is implemented in compliance with the required level of prudence.	**Practice M-3.1** The asset management team operates in a sustainable, balanced, and cohesive manner.	**Practice M-3.2** The investment system is defined, focused, and consistently adds value.
Practice M-4.3 Control procedures are in place to periodically review policies for best execution, "soft dollars," and proxy voting.	**Practice M-4.4** There is a process to periodically review the organization's effectiveness in meeting its fiduciary responsibilities.	**Practice SA-4.2** Periodic reviews are made of qualitative and/or organizational changes of investment decision-makers.	**Practice SA-4.3** Control procedures are in place to periodically review policies for best execution, "soft dollars," and proxy voting.	**Practice SA-3.2** Applicable "safe harbor" provisions are followed (when elected).	**Practice SA-3.3** Investment vehicles are appropriate for the portfolio size.	**Practice M-3.3** The investment research process is defined, focused, and documented.	**Practice M-3.4** The portfolio management process for each distinct strategy is clearly defined, focused, and documented.
		Practice SA-4.4 Fees for investment management are consistent with agreements and with all applicable laws.	**Practice SA-4.5** "Finder's fees" or other forms of compensation that may have been paid for asset placement are appropriately applied, utilized, and documented.	**Practice SA-3.4** A due diligence process is followed in selecting service providers, including the custodian.		**Practice M-3.5** The trade execution process is defined, focused, and documented.	
		Practice SA-4.6 There is a process to periodically review the organization's effectiveness in meeting its fiduciary responsibilities.					

LEGEND:
Practices in gold that begin with an "SA" define a fiduciary standard of excellence for Investment Stewards and Investment Advisors.

Practices in blue that begin with an "M" define a fiduciary standard of excellence for Investment Managers.

"SA" Practices highlighted are best reviewed in conjunction with Investment Managers Practices.

IT'S ABOUT LAW

The legal *Substantiation* for each Practice is also provided. All twenty-two Practices are substantiated by legislation, case law, and/or regulatory opinion letters from:

ERISA—Employee Retirement Income Security Act (impacts qualified retirement plans)

UPIA—Uniform Prudent Investor Act (impacts private trusts)

UPMIFA—Uniform Prudent Management of Institutional Funds Act (impacts foundations, endowments, and government-sponsored charitable institutions)

MPERS—Uniform Management of Public Employee Retirement Systems Act (impacts state, county, and municipal retirement plans)

See Comments section on page 14 for more information regarding these legislative acts.

If an Investment Steward read all of these Acts and identified the common fiduciary practices the Steward would discover seven common practices. We have coined the term "Global Fiduciary Precepts" to denote these seven practices. They are:

1. **Know standards, laws, and trust provisions.**

2. **Diversify assets to specific risk/return profile of client.**

3. **Prepare investment policy statement.**

4. **Use "prudent experts" (for example, an Investment Manager) and document due diligence.**

5. **Control and account for investment expenses.**

6. **Monitor the activities of "prudent experts."**

7. **Avoid conflicts of interest and prohibited transactions.**

Anytime an investment question is raised, the Steward should map the question against the seven Global Fiduciary Precepts. For example, if a committee member were to ask: "Should we invest in a hedge fund?" The Steward should be thinking:

How would this impact the asset allocation?

Does the IPS provide for this type of investment strategy?

Do we have the resources to conduct a proper due diligence to select an appropriate hedge fund manager?

Do we have the capability to select and monitor this type of investment option?

Will the overall investment management fees rise if we participate in this type of investment strategy?

IT'S ABOUT THE "TONE AT THE TOP"

"Much has been written about 'tone at the top,' the ethical standards that Boards and chief executives set, and its importance cannot be overestimated. Organizational behavior oftentimes mirrors the standards of integrity and fair dealing (i.e., avoidance of conflicts of interests, and self entitlements) exhibited by Board members and high ranking officials."

NAVIGANT CONSULTING,
JANUARY, 2006

Investment Stewards, Investment Advisors and Investment Managers who do not foster and promote a culture of fiduciary responsibility are going to lack the sensitivity and awareness to identify the fiduciary breaches of others. When a fiduciary has its own conflicts of interests, then that fiduciary will be marginalized at best; corrupted at worst.

"Society depends upon professionals to provide reliable, fixed standards in situations where the facts are murky or the temptations too strong. Their principal contribution is an ability to bring sound judgment to bear on these situations. They represent the best a particular community is able to muster in response to new challenges."

DR. ROBERT KENNEDY,
UNIVERSITY OF ST. THOMAS

Investment fiduciaries are challenged by the need to foster a culture of fiduciary responsibility that is defined by reliable, fixed standards. The management of investment decisions is not an easy task, even for trained investment professionals; and a nearly impossible task for lay decision-makers who serve as trustees and investment committee members of retirement plans, foundations, endowments, and personal trusts. Since professional and lay decision-makers depend on an assortment of industry vendors for assistance in managing their diverse roles and responsibilities, it is important to foster and promote a culture of fiduciary responsibility with all involved parties.

IT'S ABOUT THE BENEFITS OF HAVING A DEFINED STANDARD

The twenty-two Practices are easily adaptable to all types of portfolios, regardless of size or intended use, and should:

☐ Help to establish evidence that the Steward is following a prudent investment process.

☐ Serve as a practicum for all parties involved with investment decisions (Investment Advisors, Investment Managers, accountants, and attorneys), and provide an excellent educational outline of the duties and responsibilities of Investment Stewards.

☐ Potentially help to increase long-term investment performance by identifying more appropriate procedures for:
  • Diversifying the portfolio across multiple asset classes and peer groups
  • Evaluating investment management fees and expenses
  • Selecting Investment Managers
  • Terminating Investment Managers that no longer are appropriate

☐ Help uncover investment and/or procedural risks not previously identified, which may assist in prioritizing investment management projects.

☐ Encourage Stewards to compare their practices and procedures with those of their peers.

☐ Assist in establishing benchmarks to measure the progress of the Investment Steward.

LEGAL COUNSEL'S EDITORIAL STATEMENT

The fiduciary practices described in this handbook address many of the ethical and procedural requirements of Investment Stewards. In addition, the Steward must become familiar, and comply, with all other laws applicable to the Steward's duties and responsibilities.

This handbook is not intended to be used as a source of legal advice. The Investment Steward should discuss the topics with legal counsel knowledgeable in this specific area of the law. References to laws, case law, and/or regulatory opinion letters are provided merely as substantiation to the suggested practices. Nor is this handbook intended to represent specific investment advice.

The scope of this handbook does not address: (1) financial, actuarial, and/or recordkeeping issues; (2) valuation issues of closely held stock, limited partnerships, hard assets, insurance contracts, hedge funds, or blind investment pools; and/or (3) risk management issues such as the use of derivative and/or synthetic financial instruments.

COMMENTS REGARDING THE UPIA, UPMIFA, AND MPERS

The UPIA was released by the National Conference of Commissioners on Uniform State Laws in 1994, and subsequently approved by the American Bar Association and American Bankers Association. The UPIA serves as a default statute for private trusts. Ordinarily, the provisions of a private trust prevail. If a trust document is silent regarding a particular fiduciary duty, such as the duty to diversify, then the provisions of the UPIA apply.

State Adoptions:

Alabama	Maine	Oklahoma
Alaska	Massachusetts	Oregon
Arizona	Maryland	Pennsylvania
Arkansas	Michigan	Rhode Island
California	Minnesota	South Carolina
Colorado	Mississippi	South Dakota
Connecticut	Missouri	Tennessee
District of Columbia	Montana	Texas
Hawaii	Nebraska	U.S. Virgin Islands
Idaho	Nevada	Utah
Illinois	New Hampshire	Vermont
Indiana	New Jersey	Virginia
Iowa	New Mexico	Washington
Kansas	North Carolina	West Virginia
	North Dakota	Wisconsin
	Ohio	Wyoming

In the opinion of the authors, states that have an Act substantially similar to UPIA (as it pertains to defining an investment fiduciary standard of care) are: Delaware, Florida, Georgia, and New York.

If a particular state is not identified above, then the Advisor is advised to seek the opinion of qualified legal counsel on the fiduciary standard of care that is applicable to that particular state, and whether any of the fiduciary practices covered in this handbook are not applicable.

MPERS was proposed in 1997 by the NCCUSL and may impact state, county, and municipal retirement plans. To date, Maryland and Wyoming are the only states that have formally adopted this act.

In the opinion of the authors, South Carolina has adopted an act substantially similar to MPERS (as it pertains to defining an investment fiduciary standard of care).

UPMIFA was released in July 2006 by the NCCUSL. It is now available for consideration of adoption by state legislatures. It impacts foundations, endowments, and government-sponsored charitable organizations. It is replacing UMIFA, which has been adopted by 47 states and the District of Columbia.

STEP 1: ORGANIZE

INVESTMENTS ARE MANAGED IN ACCORDANCE WITH ALL APPLICABLE LAWS, TRUST DOCUMENTS, AND WRITTEN INVESTMENT POLICY STATEMENTS (IPS).

The starting point for the Investment Steward is to collect, analyze, and review all of the documents pertaining to the establishment and management of the investments.

As in managing any financial decision, the Steward has to set definitive goals and objectives that are consistent with the portfolio's current and future resources, the limits and constraints of applicable trust documents and statutes, and, in the case of personal trusts, the needs and requirements of each beneficiary.

Proof that such a framework has been established presumes written documentation exists in some form.

Practical Application

The following documents, at a minimum, should be collected, reviewed, and analyzed:

1. A copy of the IPS, written minutes, and/or files from investment committee meetings
2. Applicable trust documents (including amendments)
3. Custodial and brokerage agreements
4. Service agreements with investment management vendors (custodian, money managers, investment consultant, actuary, accountant, and attorney)
5. Information on retained Investment Managers; specifically the ADV for each separate account manager and prospectus for each mutual fund
6. Investment performance reports from the Investment Advisor, Investment Manager(s), and/or custodian(s)
7. Information on Investment Advisor (if one is retained)

CRITERIA

1.1.1 Investments are managed in accordance with all applicable laws.

1.1.2 Investments are managed in accordance with trust documents.

1.1.3 Investments are managed in accordance with the written IPS.

1.1.4 Documents pertaining to the investment management process are filed in a centralized location.

PRACTICE S-1.1

INVESTMENTS ARE MANAGED IN ACCORDANCE WITH ALL APPLICABLE LAWS, TRUST DOCUMENTS, AND WRITTEN INVESTMENT POLICY STATEMENTS (IPS).

Substantiation

Employee Retirement Income Security Act of 1974 [ERISA]

§3(38)(C); §104(b)(4); §402(a)(1); §402(b)(1); §402(b)(2); §403(a); §404(a)(1)(D); §404(b)(2)

Regulations
29 C.F.R. §2509.75-5 FR-4; 29 C.F.R. Interpretive Bulletin 75-5; 29 C.F.R. §2509.94-2(2); 29 C.F.R. Interpretive Bulletin 94-2 (July 29, 1994)

Case Law
Morse v. New York State Teamsters Conference Pension and Retirement Fund, 580 F. Supp. 180 (W.D.N.Y. 1983), aff'd, 761 F.2d 115 (2d Cir. 1985); *Winpisinger v. Aurora Corp. of Illinois,* 456 F. Supp. 559 (N.D. Ohio 1978); *Liss v. Smith,* 991 F. Supp. 278, 1998 (S.D.N.Y. 1998); *Dardaganis v. Grace Capital, Inc.,* 664 F. Supp. 105 (S.D.N.Y. 1987), aff'd, 889 F.2d 1237 (2d Cir. 1989)

Other
Interpretive Bulletin 75-5, 29 C.F.R. §2509.75-5; Interpretive Bulletin 94-2, 29 C.F.R. §2509.94-2

Uniform Prudent Investor Act [UPIA]

§2(a) – (d); §4

Uniform Prudent Management of Institutional Funds Act [UPMIFA]

§3(b); §3(e)

Management of Public Employee Retirement Systems Act [MPERS]

§4(a) – (d); §7(6); §8(b)

THE ROLES AND RESPONSIBILITIES OF ALL INVOLVED PARTIES (FIDUCIARIES AND NON-FIDUCIARIES) ARE DEFINED, DOCUMENTED, AND ACKNOWLEDGED.

A fiduciary is defined as someone acting in a position of trust on behalf of, or for the benefit of, a third party. Fiduciary status can be difficult to determine, and is based on *facts and circumstances*. In general, the issue is whether a person has effective control or influence over substantial investment decisions. It is not uncommon for fiduciaries to be unaware of their status.

There are numerous parties involved in the investment process, and each should have their specific duties and requirements detailed in the Investment Policy Statement, or otherwise documented in writing. This ensures continuity of the investment strategy when there is turnover, helps to prevent misunderstandings between parties, and helps to prevent omission of critical functions.

Each party involved in the investment process should acknowledge their defined duties and understand their role in the process. Those designated as fiduciaries need to acknowledge their level and understanding of fiduciary responsibility.

Stewards are responsible for the general management of the investments—in essence, the management of the twenty-two *Practices* presented in this handbook. If statutes and trust provisions permit, the Steward may delegate certain decisions to professional money managers, trustees (co-fiduciaries), and/or investment advisors and consultants. But even when decisions have been delegated to a professional, a Steward can never fully abdicate these primary responsibilities:

- Determining investment goals and objectives

- Approving an appropriate asset allocation strategy

- Establishing an explicit, written investment policy consistent with identified goals and objectives

- Approving appropriate money managers, mutual funds, or other "prudent experts" to implement the investment policy

- Monitoring the activities of the overall investment program for compliance with the investment policy

- Avoiding conflicts of interest and prohibited transactions

As mentioned previously in the Comments Section on the UPIA, the provisions of the UPIA are "default" provisions; i.e. the intentions and guidelines provided by the trust maker in the trust document delegates investment responsibility to, or otherwise appoints, an Investment Advisor other than the trustee to the trust, and the document clearly directs the trustee to allow such delegation, and absolves the trustee of such responsibility, then the trust document prevails.

CRITERIA

1.2.1 The roles and responsibilities of all parties are documented in the IPS.

1.2.2 All parties demonstrate an awareness of their duties and responsibilities.

1.2.3 All parties have acknowledged their status in writing.

1.2.4 The committee has and follows a defined set of by-laws.

THE ROLES AND RESPONSIBILITIES OF ALL INVOLVED PARTIES (FIDUCIARIES AND NON-FIDUCIARIES) ARE DEFINED, DOCUMENTED, AND ACKNOWLEDGED.

Substantiation

Employee Retirement Income Security Act of 1974 [ERISA]

§3(38)(c); §402(a)(1); §402(b)(2) and (3); §403(a)(2); §404(a)(1)(B); §405(c)(1)

Case Law
Marshall v. Glass/Metal Association and Glaziers and Glassworkers Pension Plan, 507 F. Supp. 378 2 E.B.C. 1006 (D.Hawaii 1980); *Katsaros v. Cody,* 744 F.2d 270, 5 E.B.C. 1777 (2d Cir. 1984), *cert. denied, Cody v. Donovan,* 469 U.S. 1072, 105 S. Ct. 565, 83 L.Ed. 2d 506 (1984); *Marshall v. Snyder,* 1 E.B.C. 1878 (E.D.N.Y. 1979); *Donovan v. Mazzola,* 716 F.2d 1226, 4 E.B.C. 1865 (9th Cir. 1983), *cert. denied,* 464 U.S. 1040, 104 S. Ct. 704, L.Ed.2d 169 (1984); *Fink v. National Savings and Trust Company,* 772 F. 2d 951, 6 E.B.C. 2269 (D.C. Cir. 1985)

Other
Joint Committee on Taxation, *Overview of the Enforcement and Administration of the Employee Retirement and Income Security Act of 1974* (JCX-16-90, June 6, 1990)

Uniform Prudent Investor Act [UPIA]

§1(a); §2(a); §2(d); §9(a)(1) and (2)

Other
Restatement of Trusts 3d: Prudent Investor Rule §171 (1992)

Uniform Prudent Management of Institutional Funds Act [UPMIFA]

§3(b); §3(c)

Management of Public Employee Retirement Systems Act [MPERS]

§6(a) and (b); §7; §8(b)

Other
National Labor Relations Board v. Amax Coal Co., 453 U.S. 322, 101 S. Ct. 2789, 69 L.Ed. 2d 672 (1981)

Fiduciaries and parties in interest are not involved in self-dealing.

The fundamental duty of the Investment Steward is to manage investment decisions for the exclusive benefit of another party (for example the retirement plan participant or the trust beneficiary). In addition, the Steward has a responsibility to employ an objective independent due diligence process at all times. If a participant or beneficiary is harmed by a decision not conducted at arms length, then a breach is likely to have occurred.

If a Steward even suspects he or she may have a conflict of interest—they probably do. The best advice is to end the relationship, or avoid it in the first place.

The Investment Steward should always be asking: Who benefits most from an investment decision? If the answer is any party other than the participant or the beneficiary, then the Steward is likely to be committing a fiduciary breach.

The Investment Steward should have defined policies and procedures to manage potential conflicts of interests. Special concerns are raised and additional scrutiny may be required when:

- An Investment Manager or Investment Advisor is associated with a custodian, broker-dealer, and/or shareholder services firm.

- An Investment Manager is acting as a subadvisor to a separately managed account (wrap fee account) and is required to direct trades to a particular broker-dealer.

- An Investment Manager accepts an unusually large number of directed brokerage and commission recapture mandates.

- An Investment Steward uses the assets of a public retirement plan to invest in local high-risk business ventures.

Examples of possible breaches:

- If a friend, business associate, and/or relative stands to benefit at the expense of a participant or beneficiary.

- An Investment Steward uses the assets of a private trust to provide unsecured loans to related parties and/or entities of the trustee.

- An Investment Steward hires an Investment Manager for a reason other than qualified merit.

- An Investment Manager uses "soft dollars" for any purpose other than the purchase of investment research.

- An Investment Steward uses a company retirement plan as collateral for a line of credit.

- An Investment Steward buys artwork and/or other collectibles with retirement plan assets, and puts the collectibles on display.

CRITERIA

1.3.1 Policies and procedures for overseeing and managing potential conflicts of interests are defined.

1.3.2 All fiduciaries annually acknowledge the organization's ethics policies and agree to disclose any potential conflicts of interest.

PRACTICE S-1.3

FIDUCIARIES AND PARTIES IN INTEREST ARE NOT INVOLVED IN SELF-DEALING.

Substantiation

Internal Revenue Code of 1986, as amended [IRC]

§4975

Employee Retirement Income Security Act of 1974 [ERISA]

§3(14)(A) and (B); §404(a)(1)(A); §406(a) and (b)

Case Law
Whitfield v. Tomasso, 682 F. Supp. 1287, 9 E.B.C. 2438 (E.D.N.Y 1988)

Other
DOL Advisory Council on Employee Welfare and Benefit Plans Report of the Working Group on Soft Dollars and Commission Recapture November 13, 1997

Uniform Prudent Investor Act [UPIA]

§2; §5

Uniform Prudent Management of Institutional Funds Act [UPMIFA]

Prefacatory Note

Management of Public Employee Retirement Systems Act [MPERS]

§7(1) and (2); §17(c)(12) and (13)

Other

Forbes, "Pay for Play," Sept 4, 2000; *Plan Sponsor,* "Fiduciary Fundamentals" May 5, 2000; *Fortune,* "The Seamy Side of Pension Funds," Aug 12, 2002

SERVICE AGREEMENTS AND CONTRACTS ARE IN WRITING, AND DO NOT CONTAIN PROVISIONS THAT CONFLICT WITH FIDUCIARY STANDARDS OF CARE.

An Investment Steward is required to prudently manage investment decisions, and should seek assistance from outside professionals such as Investment Advisors and Investment Managers if the Steward lacks the requisite knowledge (assuming trust documents permit the delegation of investment responsibilities).

The Steward should take reasonable steps to protect the portfolio from losses, and to avoid misunderstandings when hiring such professionals. Therefore, Stewards should reduce any agreement of substance to writing in order to define the scope of the parties' duties and responsibilities, to ensure that the portfolio is managed in accordance with the written documents that govern the investment strategy, and to confirm that the parties have a clear, mutual understanding of their roles and responsibilities.

CRITERIA

1.4.1 Agreements and contracts are periodically reviewed to ensure consistency with the needs of the managed assets.

1.4.2 Agreements and contracts are periodically reviewed by legal counsel.

1.4.3 Consideration is given to putting vendor contracts back out for bid every three years.

Substantiation

Employee Retirement Income Security Act of 1974 [ERISA]

§3(14)(B) and (38)(C); §3(38)(C); §402(c)(2); §403(a)(2); §404(a)(1); §408(b)(2)

Case Law
Liss v. Smith, 991 F. Supp. 278 (S.D.N.Y. 1998); *Whitfield v. Tomasso*, 682 F. Supp. 1287, 9 E.B.C. 2438 (E.D.N.Y. 1988)

Other
Interpretive Bulletin 94-2, 29 C.F.R. §2509.94-2

Uniform Prudent Investor Act [UPIA]

§2(a); §5; §7; §9(a)(2)

Uniform Prudent Management of Institutional Funds Act [UPMIFA]

§3(b); §3(c); §5(a)

Management of Public Employee Retirement Systems Act [MPERS]

§5(a)(2); §6(b)(2); §7

PRACTICE S-1.5

The Investment Steward has the responsibility to safeguard entrusted assets, which includes keeping the assets within the purview of the appropriate judicial system. This provides a regulatory agency the ability to seize the assets if, in its determination, it is in the best interest of the beneficiaries and/or participants.

CRITERIA

1.5.1 Assets are within the purview of the relevant judicial system.

1.5.2 ERISA plans have the required surety bond.

Substantiation

Employee Retirement Income Security Act of 1974 [ERISA]

§ 404(b); § 412(a)

Regulations
29 C.F.R. §2550.404b-1

Case Law
Varity Corporation v. Howe, 516 U.S. 489, 116 S. Ct. 1065, 134 L.Ed.2d 130 (1996)

Other
H.R. Report No. 93-1280 (93rd Congress, 2d Session, August 12, 1974)

Uniform Prudent Investor Act [UPIA]

§2(a); §5; §9(d)

Uniform Prudent Management of Institutional Funds Act [UPMIFA]

§3(b); §5(d)

Management of Public Employee Retirement Systems Act [MPERS]

§2(21); §6(e); §7; §11(c) and Comments

Step 2: Formalize

AN INVESTMENT TIME HORIZON HAS BEEN IDENTIFIED.

One of the most important decisions the Steward has to manage is the determination of the portfolio's time horizon. Time horizon being that point-in-time when more money is flowing out of the portfolio than is coming in from contributions and/or from portfolio growth.

In order to determine a portfolio's time horizon, the Investment Steward should prepare a schedule of the portfolio's anticipated cash flows. One of the fundamental duties of every Steward is to ensure that there are sufficient liquid assets to pay bills and liabilities when they come due. Also, in the case of a foundation or endowment, to provide a specified level of support when it has been promised.

Based on the time horizon, the Steward then can determine which asset classes can be appropriately considered, and what the allocation should be between the selected asset classes. A short time horizon typically is implemented with fixed income and cash, while a long investment time horizon can be prudently implemented across most asset classes.

A cash flow schedule provides the Steward with information to more effectively rebalance a portfolio's asset allocation strategy. For example, if a particular asset class is outside the range of the investment policy statement's strategic limit, one could use the cash flow information to effectively rebalance the portfolio.

CRITERIA

2.1.1 Sources, timing, distribution, and uses of cash flows are documented.

2.1.2 In the case of a defined benefit retirement plan, the appropriate asset/liability study has been factored into the time horizon.

2.1.3 In the case of a foundation or endowment, the receipt and disbursement of gifts and grants has been factored into the time horizon.

2.1.4 In the case of a retail investor, the appropriate needs-based analysis has been factored into the time horizon.

2.1.5 Sufficient liquid assets for contingency plans are maintained.

AN INVESTMENT TIME HORIZON HAS BEEN IDENTIFIED.

Suggested Procedures

One of the most important decisions the Investment Steward has to determine is the time horizon of the investment strategy. Based on the time horizon, the Investment Steward then can determine: (1) The asset classes to be considered; (2) The mix among the asset classes; (3) The sub-asset classes to be considered; and, finally, (4) The money managers or mutual funds to select.

The Hierarchy of Decisions

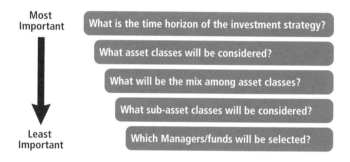

Most Important

Least Important

What is the time horizon of the investment strategy?

What asset classes will be considered?

What will be the mix among asset classes?

What sub-asset classes will be considered?

Which Managers/funds will be selected?

Substantiation

Employee Retirement Income Security Act of 1974 [ERISA]

§404(a)(1)(B)

Regulations
29 C.F.R. §2550.404a-1(b)(1)(A); 29 C.F.R. §2550.404a-1(b)(2)(A)

Case Law
Metzler v. Graham, 112 F.3d 207, E.B.C. 2857 (5th Cir. 1997)

Other
Interpretive Bulletin 96-1, 29 C.F.R. §2509.96-1; H.R. Report No. 1280, 93d Congress, 2d Session (1974)

Uniform Prudent Investor Act [UPIA]

§2(a); §2(b)

Uniform Prudent Management of Institutional Funds Act [UPMIFA]

§3

Management of Public Employee Retirement Systems Act [MPERS]

§8; §10(b)

A RISK LEVEL HAS BEEN IDENTIFIED.

The term "risk" has different connotations depending on the Investment Steward's frame of reference, circumstances, and objectives. Typically, the investment industry defines risk in terms of statistical measures such as standard deviation. However, these statistical measures may fail to adequately communicate the potential negative consequences an investment strategy can have on the Steward's ability to meet investment objectives.

An investment strategy can fail by being too conservative as well as too aggressive. A Steward could adopt a very safe investment strategy by keeping a portfolio in cash, but then see the portfolio's purchasing power whither under inflation. Or a Steward could implement a long-term growth strategy that overexposes a portfolio to equities, when a more conservative fixed-income strategy would have been sufficient to cover the identified goals and objectives.

Substantiation

Employee Retirement Income Security Act of 1974 [ERISA]

§404(a)(1)(B)

Regulations
29 C.F.R. §2550.404a-1(b)(1)(A); 29 C.F.R. §2550.404a-1(b)(2)(B)(i-iii)

Case Law
Laborers National Pension Fund v. Northern Trust Quantitative Advisors, Inc., 173 F.3d 313, 23 E.B.C. 1001 (5th Cir.), *reh'g and reh'g en banc denied,* 184 F.3d 820 (5th Cir.), *cert. denied,* 528 U.S. 967, 120 S.Ct. 406, 145 L.Ed.2d 316 (1999); *Chase v. Pevear,* 383 Mass. 350, 419 N.E.2d 1358 (1981)

Uniform Prudent Investor Act [UPIA]

§2(b) and (c); §2 Comments

Uniform Prudent Management of Institutional Funds Act [UPMIFA]

§3(e)

Management of Public Employee Retirement Systems Act [MPERS]

§8(b); §8 Comments

CRITERIA

2.2.1 The level of risk the portfolio is exposed to is understood, and the quantitative and qualitative factors that were considered are documented.

2.2.2 A "worst case" scenario has been considered, and it has been determined that the portfolio has sufficient liquidity to meet short-term (less than five years) obligations.

PRACTICE S-2.3

AN EXPECTED, MODELED RETURN TO MEET INVESTMENT OBJECTIVES HAS BEEN IDENTIFIED.

CRITERIA

2.3.1 The "expected" or "modeled" return is consistent with the portfolio's goals and objectives.

2.3.2 The "expected" or "modeled" return assumptions for each asset class are based on reasonable risk-premium assumptions, as opposed to recent short-term performance.

2.3.3 For Defined Benefit plans, the expected return values being used for actuarial calculations are reasonable.

There is no requirement or expectation that the Investment Steward forecast future returns. Rather, the Steward is required to state the presumptions that are being used to model the probable outcomes of a given investment strategy.

In this context, the term "model" means to replicate: to determine the expected returns of an investment strategy given current and historical information.

The Steward should determine whether trust documents, spending policies, and/or actuarial reports (for defined benefit retirement plans) establish a minimum investment return expectation or requirement. In all cases, the Steward should determine the expected return a given investment strategy is designed to produce.

Substantiation

Employee Retirement Income Security Act of 1974 [ERISA]

§404(a)(1)(A) and (B)

Regulations
29 C.F.R. §2550.404a-1(b)(1)(A); 29 C.F.R. §2550.404a-1(b)(2)(A)

Case Law
Federal Power Commission v. Hope Natural Gas Company, 320 U.S. 591, 64 S.Ct. 281, 88 L.Ed. 333 (1944); *Communications Satellite Corporation v. Federal Communications Commission*, 611 F.2d 883 (D.C. Cir. 1977); *Tennessee Gas Pipeline Company v. Federal Energy Regulatory Commission*, 926 F.2d 1206 (D.C. Cir. 1991)

Uniform Prudent Investor Act [UPIA]

§2(b); §2(c)(1-8)

Uniform Prudent Management of Institutional Funds Act [UPMIFA]

§3(e)

Management of Public Employee Retirement Systems Act [MPERS]

§8(a)(1)(A-F); §8(b)

SELECTED ASSET CLASSES ARE CONSISTENT WITH THE RISK, RETURN, AND TIME HORIZON.

The Investment Steward's role is to choose the appropriate combination of asset classes that optimize the identified risk and return objectives, and is consistent with the portfolio's time horizon.

The acronym "TREAT" helps to define the key inputs to an asset allocation strategy.

Asset Allocation Variables

T	Time Horizon
R	Risk Tolerance
E	Expected Return
A	Asset Class Preference
T	Tax Status

Substantiation

Employee Retirement Income Security Act of 1974 [ERISA]

§404(a)(1)(B)

Regulations
29 C.F.R. §2550.404a-1; 29 C.F.R. §2550.404a-1(b)(1)(A); 29 C.F.R. §2550.404a-1(b)(2)(B)(i-iii)

Case Law
GIW Industries, Inc. v. Trevor, Stewart, Burton & Jacobsen, Inc., 895 F.2d 729 (11th Cir. 1990); *Leigh v. Engle*, 858 F.2d 361 (7th Cir. 1988)

Other
Interpretive Bulletin 96-1, 29 C.F.R. §2509.96-1

Uniform Prudent Investor Act [UPIA]

§2(b)

Uniform Prudent Management of Institutional Funds Act [UPMIFA]

§3

Management of Public Employee Retirement Systems Act [MPERS]

§8(b)

CRITERIA

2.4.1 Assets are appropriately diversified to conform to the specified time horizon and risk/return profile.

2.4.2 For participant directed plans, selected asset classes provide each participant the ability to diversify their portfolio appropriately given their time horizon and risk/return profile.

2.4.3 The methodology and tools used to establish appropriate portfolio diversification are effective and consistently applied.

PRACTICE S-2.5

There is no formula the Investment Steward can follow to determine the best number of asset classes—the appropriate number is determined by facts and circumstances. How many asset classes should be considered? Or in the case of participant-directed retirement plans, how many investment options should be offered?

The answer is dependent on certain variables:

- Size of the portfolio

- Investment expertise of the investment decision-makers

- Ability of the decision-makers to properly monitor the strategies and/or investment options

- Sensitivity to investment expenses—more asset classes and/or options may mean higher portfolio expenses. The additional costs of added diversification should be evaluated in light of the price the fiduciary pays for being less-diversified

The Steward's choice of asset classes and their subsequent weighting within the allocation strategy will have more impact on the long-term performance of the investment portfolio than any other decision.

Substantiation

Employee Retirement Income Security Act of 1974 [ERISA]

§404(a)(1)(C)

Other
H.R. Report No. 1280, 93rd Congress, 2d Sess.304, reprinted in 1974 U.S. Code Cong. & Admin. News 5038 (1974)

Uniform Prudent Investor Act [UPIA]

§2(b)

Other
Restatement of Trusts 3d: Prudent Investor Rule §227, comment

Uniform Prudent Management of Institutional Funds Act [UPMIFA]

§3(e)

Management of Public Employee Retirement Systems Act [MPERS]

§8(a)(1); §8(a)(4); §10(2)

CRITERIA

2.5.1 Individuals responsible for implementing and monitoring investment decisions have the time, inclination, and knowledge to do so effectively.

2.5.2 The process and tools used to implement and monitor investments in the selected asset classes are effective.

2.5.3 The ability to access suitable investment products within all selected asset classes has been considered.

THERE IS AN IPS WHICH CONTAINS THE DETAIL TO DEFINE, IMPLEMENT, AND MANAGE A SPECIFIC INVESTMENT STRATEGY.

The preparation and maintenance of the IPS is one of the most critical functions of the Investment Steward. The IPS should be viewed as the business plan and the essential management tool for directing and communicating the activities of the portfolio. It is a formal, long-range, strategic plan that allows the Steward to coordinate the management of the investment program in a logical and consistent framework. All material investment facts, assumptions, and opinions should be included.

The IPS should have sufficient detail that a third party would be able to implement the investment strategy; be flexible enough that it can be implemented in a complex and dynamic financial environment; and yet not be so detailed it requires constant revisions and updates. Addendums should be used to identify information that will change on a more frequent basis such as the names of board members, accountants, attorneys, actuaries, and Investment Managers; and the capital markets assumptions used to develop the plan's asset allocation.

The Steward is required to manage investment decisions with a reasonable level of detail. By reducing that detail to writing (i.e., preparing a written IPS) the Steward can: (1) avoid unnecessary differences of opinion and the resulting conflicts; (2) minimize the possibility of missteps due to a lack of clear guidelines; (3) establish a reasoned basis for measuring their compliance; and (4) establish and communicate reasonable and clear expectations with participants, beneficiaries, and investors.

One of the challenges of writing an IPS is to create investment guidelines specific enough to clearly establish the parameters of the desired investment process, yet provide enough latitude so as not to create an oversight burden. This is particularly true when establishing the portfolio's asset allocation and rebalancing limits.

Rebalancing is required to maintain proper diversification, where the goal is to ensure that the portfolio does not stray far from its targeted levels of risk and return. An optimal portfolio only can be maintained by periodically rebalancing the portfolio to maintain the intended diversification.

A well-written IPS can serve to insulate the Investment Steward from the temptation to chase the latest top-performing asset class or "hottest" Investment Manager. By establishing specific asset allocation parameters and money manager (or mutual fund) selection criteria, it is much easier to determine whether a prospective manager fits into the approved investment program.

The Steward should investigate the qualities, characteristics, and merits of each Investment Manager and identify the role each plays in the implementation of the investment strategy. However, such an investigation and the related analysis cannot be conducted in a vacuum—it must be within the context of the needs of the investment strategy. Once the needs have been defined and the general strategies developed, specific Investment Managers should be chosen within the context of this strategy.

CRITERIA

2.6.1 The IPS defines the duties and responsibilities of all parties involved.

2.6.2 The IPS defines diversification and rebalancing guidelines consistent with specified risk, return, time horizon, and cash flow parameters.

2.6.3 The IPS defines due diligence criteria for selecting investment options.

2.6.4 The IPS defines monitoring criteria for investment options and service vendors.

2.6.5 The IPS defines procedures for controlling and accounting for investment expenses.

THERE IS AN IPS WHICH CONTAINS THE DETAIL TO DEFINE, IMPLEMENT, AND MANAGE A SPECIFIC INVESTMENT STRATEGY.

The fiduciary duty to monitor the performance of Investment Managers and other service providers is inherent in the obligations of Stewards to act prudently in carrying out their duties. Specific performance criteria and objectives should be identified for each Investment Manager.

The Steward must establish procedures for controlling and accounting for investment expenses in order to fulfill the obligation to manage investment decisions with the requisite level of care, skill, and prudence; and to fulfill the specific obligation of the fiduciary to pay only reasonable and necessary expenses.

Substantiation

Employee Retirement Income Security Act of 1974 [ERISA]

§402(c)(3); §404(a); §406(a)(1)(C); §408(b)(2)

Regulations
29 C.F.R. §2550.404a-1(b)(1)(A); §2550.404a-1(b)(2)(i); 29 C.F.R. §2550.404a-1(b)(2)

Case Law
In re Unisys Savings Plan Litigation, 74 F.3d 420, 19 E.B.C. 2393 (3rd Cir.), *cert. denied,* 510 U.S. 810, 117 S.Ct. 56, 136 L.Ed.2d 19 (1996); *Morrissey v. Curran,* 567 F.2d 546, 1 E.B.C. 1659 (2nd Cir. 1977); *Harley v. Minnesota Mining and Manufacturing Company,* 42 F. Supp.2d 898 (D.Minn. 1999), aff'd, 284 F.3d 901 (8th Cir. 2002); *Whitfield v. Cohen,* 682 F. Supp. 188, 9 E.B.C. 1739 (S.D.N.Y. 1988); *Liss v. Smith,* 991 F.Supp. 278 (S.D.N.Y. 1988); *Leigh v. Engle,* 858 F.2d 361, 10 E.B.C. 1041 (7th Cir. 1988), *cert. denied,* 489 U.S. 1078, 109 S.Ct. 1528, 103 L.Ed.2d 833 (1989)

Other
Interpretive Bulletin 94-2, 29 C.F.R. §2509.94-2; Interpretive Bulletin 75-8, 29 C.F.R. §2509.75-8; Interpretive Bulletin 96-1, 29 C.F.R. §2509.96-1(e); H.R. Report No. 1280, 93rd Cong. 2d Sess. 304, reprinted in 1974 U.S. Code Cong. & Admin. News 5038 (1974)

THERE IS AN IPS WHICH CONTAINS THE DETAIL TO DEFINE, IMPLEMENT, AND MANAGE A SPECIFIC INVESTMENT STRATEGY.

Uniform Prudent Investor Act [UPIA]

§2(a-b); §2 Comments; §3 and Comments; §4; §7; §9(a)(1), (2) and (3)

Other
Restatement of Trusts 3d: Prudent Investor Rule §227(a); OCC Interpretive Letter No. 722 (March 12, 1996), citing the Restatement of Trusts 3d: Prudent Investor Rule §227, comment m at 58 (1992)

Uniform Prudent Management of Institutional Funds Act [UPMIFA]

§3(c) §3(e) §5(a)

Management of Public Employee Retirement Systems Act [MPERS]

§6(b)(2) and (3); 7(2), (3) and (5); §7(5) and Comments; §8(a); §8 and Comments

Other
Restatement of Trusts 3d: Prudent Investor Rule §227, comment g

PRACTICE S-2.7

THE IPS DEFINES APPROPRIATELY STRUCTURED, SOCIALLY RESPONSIBLE INVESTMENT (SRI) STRATEGIES (WHERE APPLICABLE).

There is an increasing interest by Investment Stewards to incorporate social, ethical, moral, and/or religious criteria into their investment strategy. The desire is to align investment decisions with the core values of the organization, sponsor, donor, or grantor. There are three terms that are used interchangeably by the industry: mission-based investing, socially responsible investing (SRI); and environmental; social; and governance (ESG) considerations.

No matter how worthwhile or well-intended, fiduciary standards of care cannot be abrogated to accommodate the pursuit of an SRI strategy. As a general rule, any restriction on an investment program has the potential to reduce the portfolio's total return—itself a breach of fiduciary responsibility.

The key to successfully incorporating an SRI strategy is for the Investment Steward to demonstrate that prospective investment results are not negatively impacted. It has become a generally accepted practice to permit the inclusion of an SRI strategy as a secondary screen to a normal (unrestricted) investment process. However, if there are equally attractive investment options, then social factors may be considered.

For Stewards guided by the UPIA, there may be three notable exceptions to the above:

1. The trust documents establishing the private trust, foundation, or endowment prefers the use of SRI.

2. A donor directs the use of an SRI Strategy.

3. A reasonable person would deduce from the foundation's/endowment's mission that SRI would be adopted (e.g., it is reasonable to assume that the American Cancer Society would avoid investing in tobacco companies).

THE IPS DEFINES APPROPRIATELY STRUCTURED, SOCIALLY RESPONSIBLE INVESTMENT (SRI) STRATEGIES (WHERE APPLICABLE).

Substantiation

Employee Retirement Income Security Act of 1974 [ERISA]

§403(c)(1); §404(a)(1)

Other
ERISA Opinion Letter 98-04A (May 28, 1998); Interpretive Bulletin 94-1, 29 C.F.R. §2509.94-1

Uniform Prudent Investor Act [UPIA]

§403(c)(1); §404(a)(1)

Uniform Prudent Management of Institutional Funds Act [UPMIFA]

§3(b); §3(e)

Management of Public Employee Retirement Systems Act [MPERS]

§7(1), (2) and (3); §8(a) (1) and (2); §8(a)(5); §8(b)

United Nations' Principles for Responsible Investment

In 2005, the United Nations Secretary-General convened an international group of institutional investors to reflect on the increasing relevance of ESG issues to investment practices. The outgrowth of the study was the release of the six "Principles for Responsible Investment":

1. We will incorporate ESG issues into investment analysis and decision-making processes.

2. We will be active owners and incorporate ESG issues into our ownership policies and practices.

3. We will seek appropriate disclosure on ESG issues by the entities in which we invest.

4. We will promote acceptance and implementation of the Principles within the investment industry.

5. We will work together to enhance our effectiveness in implementing the Principles.

6. We will each report on our activities and progress towards implementing the Principles.

STEP 3: IMPLEMENT

PRACTICE S-3.1

THE INVESTMENT STRATEGY IS IMPLEMENTED IN COMPLIANCE WITH THE REQUIRED LEVEL OF PRUDENCE.

CRITERIA

3.1.1 A due diligence procedure for selecting investment options exists.

3.1.2 The due diligence process is consistently applied.

In most cases, Stewards are not expressly required to use professional money managers. However, Investment Stewards will likely be held to the same expert standard of care, and their activities and conduct will be measured against those of investment professionals.*

The prudent Steward is strongly encouraged to delegate investment decisions to professionals when lacking the requisite expertise.

SUGGESTED FIELDS OF DUE DILIGENCE	Threshold Defined by fi360	Threshold Defined by Fiduciary	IPS (Practice 2.6)	Implement (Practice 3.1)	Monitor (Practice 4.1)
			Due diligence is reflected in procedures		
1. Regulatory oversight	Each investment option should be managed by: (a) a bank, (b) an insurance company, (c) a registered investment company (mutual fund), or (d) a registered investment adviser.				
2. Minimum track record	Each investment option should have at least three years of history so that performance statistics can be properly calculated.				
3. Stability of the organization	The same portfolio management team should be in place for at least two years.				
4. Assets in the product	Each investment option should have at least $75 million under management (for mutual funds - can include assets in related share classes).				
5. Holdings consistent with style	At least 80% of the underlying securities should be consistent with the broad asset class.				
6. Correlation to style or peer group	Each investment option should be highly correlated to the asset class being implemented.				
7. Expense ratios/fees	Fees should not be in the bottom quartile (most expensive) of the peer group.				
8. Performance relative to assumed risk	The investment option's risk - adjusted performance (Alpha and/or Sharpe Ratio) should be evaluated against the peer group median manager's risk-adjusted performance.				
9. Performance relative to a peer group	Each investment option's performance should be evaluated against the peer group's median manager return, for 1-, 3-, and 5-year cumulative periods.				
10. Other					
11. Other					

THE INVESTMENT STRATEGY IS IMPLEMENTED IN COMPLIANCE WITH THE REQUIRED LEVEL OF PRUDENCE.

Substantiation

Employee Retirement Income Security Act of 1974 [ERISA]

§402(c)(3); §403(a)(1) and (2); §404(a)(1)(B)

Regulations
29 C.F.R. §2550.404a-1(b)(1) and (2)

Case Law
772 F.2d 951 (D.C. Cir. 1985); *Katsaros v. Cody,* 744 F.2d 270,5 E.B.C. 1777 (2nd Cir.), *cert. denied,* 469 U.S. 1072, 105S.Ct. 565, 83 L.Ed.2d 506 (1984); *Donovan v. Mazzola,* 716 F.2d 1226 (9th Cir. 1983), *cert. denied,* 464 U.S. 1040, 104 S.Ct. 704, 79 L.Ed.2d 169 (1984); *United States v. MasonTenders Dist. Council of Greater New York,* 909 F. Supp. 882,19 E.B.C. 1467 (S.D.N.Y. 1995); *Trapani v. Consolidated Edison Employees' Mutual Aid Society,* 693 F. Supp. 1509 (S.D.N.Y. 1988)

Uniform Prudent Investor Act [UPIA]

§2(c); §2(f); §9(a)(1-3)

Uniform Prudent Management of Institutional Funds Act [UPMIFA]

§3(b); 5(a)

Management of Public Employee Retirement Systems Act[MPERS]

§6(a); §6(b)(1); §6(b)(3); §7(3); §8(a)(1)

---

* *A professional who receives compensation as a trustee or holds themself out as possessing skills comparable to those of a professional trustee is held to a prudent expert standard of care. Although a court may not find a lay trustee financially liable in the same manner as a professional trustee, the court could find a cause for dismissing the trustee from his or her duties. In the case where the lay trustee held themself out as having appropriate skills, the court would likely hold even the lay trustee to an expert standard of care.*

PRACTICE S-3.2

APPLICABLE "SAFE HARBOR" PROVISIONS ARE FOLLOWED (WHEN ELECTED).

There are three important concepts associated with each of the "safe harbor" procedures summarized in this Practice:

1. They are voluntary—the procedures are not compulsory for the Steward. However, a Steward choosing not to seek an available "safe harbor" bears all the risks and consequences.

2. They may insulate the Steward from liability associated with certain investment-related decisions and acts. The Steward should think of "safe harbor" procedures as a form of "insurance."

3. They require the Steward to demonstrate compliance with the defined requirements. (The question of "literal" versus "substantial" compliance will be answered by the courts.)

There are three distinct "safe harbors" available to Investment Stewards:

1. The Committee-Directed "Safe Harbor"

2. The Participant-Directed "Safe Harbor" [also known as 404(c)] (applicable only to ERISA Investment Stewards)

3. The Fiduciary Adviser "Safe Harbor" (applicable only to ERISA Investment Stewards)

Committee-Directed "Safe Harbor" Requirements

When investment decisions are committee-directed, which is often the case for defined benefit plans, foundations, and endowments; there are five generally recognized "safe harbor" requirements.

1. Investment decisions must be delegated to a "prudent expert(s)" (registered investment adviser [including mutual funds], bank, or insurance company).

2. The Investment Steward must demonstrate that the prudent expert(s) was selected by following a due diligence process.

3. The prudent expert(s) must be given discretion over the assets.

4. The prudent expert(s) must acknowledge their co-fiduciary status in writing (mutual funds are exempted from this requirement—the prospectus is deemed to serve as the fund's fiduciary acknowledgment).

5. The Investment Steward must monitor the activities of the prudent expert(s) to ensure that the expert(s) is properly performing the agreed upon tasks using the agreed upon criteria.

APPLICABLE "SAFE HARBOR" PROVISIONS ARE FOLLOWED (WHEN ELECTED).

Participant-Directed "Safe Harbor" Requirements [also known as 404(c)]

When investment decisions are participant-directed, as in the case of the typical 401(k) plan, there are nine requirements. These safe harbor requirements are more commonly referred to as 404(c) requirements. There are several proposed amendments to these procedures which have been introduced by the 2006 Pension Protection Act (PPA).

The first five requirements are identical to those of the committee-directed safe harbor, a point that should not be lost on plan fiduciaries. Many 401(k) Investment Stewards have mistakenly assumed that they were relieved of many (if not all) of their fiduciary responsibilities when they elected to allow participants to manage their own investment decisions. This simply is not the case.

Requirements 1 – 5 (see above), same as for committee-directed investment decisions

6. Plan participants must be notified in writing that the plan sponsor intends to constitute a 404(c) plan, and seek liability relief through these safe harbor procedures.

7. Participants must be offered at least three investment options with materially different risk/return profiles.

    [Proposed by the PPA] As an alternative, the plan sponsor can offer participants who do not provide the plan sponsor investment direction a "qualified default investment alternative" defined as:

    A. Age-based life-cycle or targeted retirement date funds or accounts;

    B. Risk-based, balanced funds

    C. An investment management service.

    [Technical note: The above "qualified default investment alternatives" is considered "safe harbor-like" and can be offered even if the plan sponsor does not intend to constitute a 404(c) plan.]

    Employer stock is permissible if: (1) the stock is held or acquired by a registered investment company or pooled investment vehicle that is independent of the employer; or, (2) the stock is acquired as a matching contribution from the employer and the stock is held at the direction of the participant.

Applicable "safe harbor" provisions are followed (when elected).

8. Participants must receive information and education on the different investment options.

   [Proposed by the PPA] When a "qualified default investment alternative" is offered, the participant must be provided details of the "alternative" and how to obtain additional information on the option.

9. Participants must be provided the opportunity to change their investment strategy/allocation with a frequency that is appropriate in light of market volatility.

   [Proposed by the PPA] When a "qualified default investment alternative" is offered, the participant must be provided a "notification" 30 days in advance of the first investment; and within at least 30 days in advance of each subsequent year; of the opportunity to transfer assets to any other investment alternative available without financial penalty.

Fiduciary Adviser "Safe Harbor" Requirements

The Act introduces a new safe harbor for Investment Stewards who want to provide specific investment advice to 401(k) plan participants, and introduces two new terms that are related to the safe harbor requirements: "fiduciary adviser" and "eligible investment advice arrangement":

A "fiduciary adviser" is a person who is providing specific investment advice to plan participants.

An "eligible investment advice arrangement," is either a computer-driven advice model and/or is fee neutral. (The fiduciary adviser's compensation is not impacted by which fund family, fund, share class, and/or asset mix is suggested.)

The new fiduciary adviser safe harbor requirements are:

1. The Investment Steward must prudently select a qualified fiduciary adviser.

2. The fiduciary adviser must acknowledge, to the Investment Steward and each participant, fiduciary status in writing, disclose all conflicts of interests, and all forms of compensation.

3. The Investment Steward must determine that the fiduciary adviser's "eligible investment advice arrangement," including the associated fees and expenses, is appropriate for the plan's participants.

4. The Investment Steward must prudently monitor the fiduciary adviser, and ensure that both the procedural prudence of the fiduciary adviser, and the "eligible investment advice arrangement," are audited on an annual basis.

APPLICABLE "SAFE HARBOR" PROVISIONS ARE FOLLOWED (WHEN ELECTED).

Substantiation

Employee Retirement Income Security Act of 1974 [ERISA]

§402(c)(3); §404(a) and (c); §404(c)(4); §404(c)(5); §405(d)(1)

Regulations
29 C.F.R. §2550.404a-1; 29 C.F.R. §2550.404a-1(b)(1) and (2)

Case Law
Tittle v. Enron Corp., 284 F.Supp.2d 511, 578 (S.D. Texas 2003)

Other
Interpretive Bulletin 75-8, 29 C.F.R. §2509.75-8 (FR-17Q); Interpretive Bulletin 94-2, 29 C.F.R. §2509.94-2; DOL Miscellaneous Document, 4/13/98 – Study of 401(k) Plan Fees and Expenses; Fed. Reg., Vol. 44, p. 37255

Uniform Prudent Investor Act [UPIA]

§9(a); §9(c)

Uniform Prudent Management of Institutional Funds Act [UPMIFA]

§5(a); 5(c)

Management of Public Employee Retirement Systems Act [MPERS]

§6(b); §6(d)

PRACTICE S-3.3

INVESTMENT VEHICLES ARE APPROPRIATE FOR THE PORTFOLIO SIZE.

CRITERIA

3.3.1 Decisions regarding passive and active investment strategies are documented and appropriately implemented.

3.3.2 Decisions regarding the use of separately managed and commingled accounts, such as mutual funds and unit trusts, are documented and appropriately implemented.

3.3.3 Regulated investment options are selected over unregulated options when comparable risk and return characteristics are projected.

3.3.4 Investment options that are covered by readily available data sources are selected over similar alternatives for which limited coverage is available.

3.3.5 In the case of wrap or sub-accounts, the portfolio's return is comparable to the returns received by institutional clients in the same investment strategy.

The primary focus of this Practice is the implementation of the investment strategy with appropriate investment vehicles.

It is important for the Steward to be familiar with the universe of available investment options (mutual funds, ETFs, and separate account managers to illustrate the more common vehicles), for no one implementation structure is right for all occasions.

There are numerous factors that should be considered in the selection of an investment vehicle, including:

- Ease of liquidity
- Minimum required investment
- The degree to which the investment is diversified
- Ease in meeting asset allocation and rebalancing guidelines
- Ability to perform the appropriate due diligence
- Flexibility in adjusting fees for growing or larger portfolios
- Ability to fund with assets-in-kind
- Built-in (phantom) tax issues
- Tax efficiency – ability to manage the tax consequences of low-basis and/or restricted stock
- Flexibility in year-end tax planning
- Degree of portfolio transparency
- Whether portfolio and performance information is audited
- Degree of regulatory oversight
- Ability to give investment direction to the portfolio manager
- Deductibility of management fees

INVESTMENT VEHICLES ARE APPROPRIATE FOR THE
PORTFOLIO SIZE.

Substantiation

Employee Retirement Income Security Act of 1974 [ERISA]

§404(a)(1)(B); §404(a)(1)(C)

Regulations
29 C.F.R. §2550.404c-1(b)(3)(i)(C)

Case Law
Metzler v. Graham, 112 F.3d 207, 20 E.B.C. 2857 (5th Cir. 1997); *Marshall v. Glass/Metal Ass'n and Glaziers and Glassworkers Pension Plan,* 507 F. Supp. 378 (D.Hawaii 1980); *GIW Industries, Inc. v. Trevor, Stewart, Burton & Jacobsen, Inc.,* 10 E.B.C. 2290 (S.D.Ga. 1989); *aff'd,* 895 F.2d 729 (11th Cir. 1990); *Leigh v. Engle,* 858 F.2d 361, 10 E.B.C. 1041 (7th Cir. 1988), *cert. denied,* 489 U.S. 1078, 109 S.Ct. 1528, 103 L.Ed.2d 833 (1989)

Other
H.R. Report No. 1280, 93rd Congress, 2d Sess. (1974), reprinted in 1974 U.S. Code Cong. & Admin. News 5038 (1974)

Uniform Prudent Investor Act [UPIA]

§2(a); §3; §3 Comments

Uniform Prudent Management of Institutional Funds Act [UPMIFA]

§3(e)

Management of Public Employee Retirement Systems Act [MPERS]

§7(3); §8(a)(1)

Practice S-3.4

CRITERIA

3.4.1 A documented due diligence process is applied to select the custodian and all other service providers.

3.4.2 The custodian has appropriate and adequate insurance to cover the portfolio amount.

3.4.3 An appropriate sweep money market fund is selected.

3.4.4 An inquiry has been made as to whether the custodian can facilitate performance reporting and year-end tax statements.

Custodial selection is a very important fiduciary function. Most Investment Stewards abdicate the decision to the Investment Advisors or Investment Managers. Yet, as with other prudent practices, there are a number of important decisions that need to be managed. The role of the custodian is to: (1) hold securities for safekeeping, (2) report on holdings and transactions, (3) collect interest and dividends, and, if required, (4) effect trades.

At the retail level, the custodian typically is a brokerage firm. Most securities are held in street name, with the assets commingled with those of the brokerage firm. To protect the assets, brokerage firms obtain adequate and appropriate insurance. Most institutional investors choose to use trust companies as custodians and pay an additional custody fee. The primary benefit is that the assets are held in a separate account, and are not commingled with other assets of the institution.

Substantiation

Employee Retirement Income Security Act of 1974 [ERISA]

§402(a)(1); §402(b)(2); §404(a)(1)(B)

Other
Interpretive Bulletin 96-1, 29 C.F.R. §2509.96-1; DOL Information Letter, Qualified Plan Services (7/28/98); DOL Information Letter, Service Employee's International Union (2/19/98)

Uniform Prudent Investor Act [UPIA]

§2(a); §7; §7 Comments; §9(a) (1), (2) and (3)

Uniform Prudent Management of Institutional Funds Act [UPMIFA]

§3(b); §3(c); §5(a)

Management of Public Employee Retirement Systems Act [MPERS]

§6(a) and (b)(1) and (2); §7

PERIODIC REPORTS COMPARE INVESTMENT PERFORMANCE AGAINST APPROPRIATE INDEX, PEER GROUP, AND IPS OBJECTIVES.

The monitoring function extends beyond a strict examination of performance. By definition, monitoring occurs across all policy and procedural issues previously addressed in this handbook. The ongoing review, analysis, and monitoring of investment decision-makers and/or money managers is just as important as the due diligence implemented during the manager selection process.

In keeping with the duty of prudence, an Investment Steward appointing an Investment Manager must determine the frequency of the reviews necessary, taking into account such factors as: (1) prevailing general economic conditions, (2) the size of the portfolio, (3) the investment strategies employed, (4) the investment objectives sought, and (5) the volatility of the investments selected.

The Steward should establish performance objectives for each Investment Manager, and record the same in the IPS. Investment performance should be evaluated in terms of an appropriate market index, and relevant peer group.

The IPS also should describe the actions to be taken when an Investment Manager fails to meet established criteria. The Steward should acknowledge that fluctuating rates of return characterize the securities markets, and may cause variations in performance. The Steward should evaluate performance from a long-term perspective.

There often will be times when an Investment Manager is beginning to exhibit shortfalls in the defined performance objectives but, in the opinion of the Steward, does not warrant termination. In such situations, the Steward should establish in the IPS specific "watch list" procedures. The decision to retain or terminate a manager cannot be made by a formula. It is the Steward's confidence in the Investment Manager's ability to perform in the future that ultimately determines the retention of the Investment Manager.

CRITERIA

4.1.1 The performance of each investment option is periodically compared against an appropriate index, peer group, and due diligence procedures defined in the IPS.

4.1.2 The information that is provided in performance reports is evaluated and actions considered are documented.

4.1.3 "Watch list" procedures for underperforming Investment Managers are followed.

4.1.4 Rebalancing procedures are followed.

PRACTICE S-4.1

PERIODIC REPORTS COMPARE INVESTMENT PERFORMANCE AGAINST APPROPRIATE INDEX, PEER GROUP, AND IPS OBJECTIVES.

Substantiation

Employee Retirement Income Security Act of 1974 [ERISA]

§3(38); §402(c)(3)

Case Law
Leigh v. Engle, 727 F.2d 113 , 4 E.B.C. 2702(7th Cir. 1984); *Atwood v. Burlington Indus. Equity, Inc.,* 18 E.B.C. 2009 (M.D.N.C. 1994)

Other
Interpretive Bulletin 75-8, 29 C.F.R. §2509.75-8 (FR-17Q); Interpretive Bulletin 94-2, 29 C.F.R. §2509.94-2

Uniform Prudent Investor Act [UPIA]

§2(a); §9(a) (1 – 3)

Uniform Prudent Management of Institutional Funds Act [UPMIFA]

§3(b); §5(a)

Management of Public Employee Retirement Systems Act [MPERS]

§6(a) and (b)(1 – 3); §6 Comments; §6(d); §8(b)

PERIODIC REVIEWS ARE MADE OF QUALITATIVE AND/OR ORGANIZATIONAL CHANGES OF INVESTMENT DECISION-MAKERS.

The Investment Steward has a continuing duty to exercise reasonable care, skill, and caution in monitoring the performance of Investment Managers and Investment Advisor.

The Steward's review of an Investment Manager must be based on more than recent investment performance results, for all Investment Managers will experience periods of poor performance. Stewards also should not be replacing their manager lineup simply because of the reported success of other managers.

In addition to the quantitative reviews of Investment Managers, periodic reviews of the qualitative performance and/or organizational changes to the Managers should be made at reasonable intervals. On a periodic basis (for example, quarterly) the Steward should review whether each Investment Manager continues to meet specified objectives. For example:

- The Investment Manager's adherence to the guidelines established by the IPS

- Material changes in the Manager's organization, investment philosophy, and/or personnel

- Any legal or regulatory agency proceedings that may affect the Manager

Substantiation

Employee Retirement Income Security Act of 1974 [ERISA]

§3(38); §402(c)(3); §404(a)(1)(B)

Regulations
29 C.F.R. §2550.408b-2(d); 29 C.F.R. §2550.408c-2

Other
Interpretive Bulletin 75-8, 29 C.F.R. §2509.75-8; Booklet: A Look at 401(k) Plan Fees, U.S. Department of Labor, Pension and Welfare Benefits Administration

Uniform Prudent Investor Act [UPIA]

§2(a); §7; §9(a)

Uniform Prudent Management of Institutional Funds Act [UPMIFA]

§3(b); §3(c); §5(a)

Management of Public Employee Retirement Systems Act [MPERS]

§6(a) and (b)(1 - 3); §7(5)

CRITERIA

4.2.1 Periodic evaluations of qualitative factors which may impact Investment Managers and Investment Advisors are performed.

4.2.2 Unsatisfactory news regarding an Investment Manager and/or Investment Advisor is documented and appropriately acted upon.

PRACTICE S-4.3

CONTROL PROCEDURES ARE IN PLACE TO PERIODICALLY REVIEW POLICIES FOR BEST EXECUTION, "SOFT DOLLARS," AND PROXY VOTING.

The Investment Steward has a responsibility to control and account for investment expenses—that the expenses are prudent and are applied in the best interests of the participant (in the case of a retirement plan), or beneficiary (in the case of a private trust, foundation, or endowment). The Steward, therefore, must monitor the following:

- *Best execution practices are followed in securities transactions.* The Steward has a responsibility to seek confirmation that each Investment Manager is seeking best execution in trading the portfolio's securities. In seeking best execution, Investment Managers are required to shop their trades with various brokerage firms, taking into consideration: (1) commission costs, (2) an analysis of the actual execution price of the security, and (3) the quality and reliability (timing) of the trade.

- *"Soft dollars" are expended only for brokerage and research for the benefit of the investment program, and the amount is reasonable in relation to the value of such services.* Soft dollars represent the excess in commission costs: the difference between what a brokerage firm charges for a trade versus the brokerage firm's actual costs. The failure of the Steward to monitor soft dollars may subject the investment program to expenditures which yield no benefit; itself a fiduciary breach.

- *Proxies are voted in a manner most likely to preserve or enhance the value of the subject stock.* The Steward can either retain the power to vote the proxies (and maintain documentation of such activity), or instruct an Investment Manager to vote on behalf of the Steward. If the power to vote proxies is retained, it is imperative that proxies are voted and documented in a timely manner.

CRITERIA

4.3.1 Control procedures are in place to periodically review policies for best execution.

4.3.2 Control procedures are in place to periodically review policies for "soft dollars."

4.3.3 Control procedures are in place to periodically review policies for proxy voting.

Substantiation

Employee Retirement Income Security Act of 1974 [ERISA]

§3(38); §402(c)(3); §403(a)(1) and (2); §404(a)(1)(A) and (B)

Case Law
Herman v. NationsBank Trust Co., (Georgia), 126 F.3d 1354, 21 E.B.C. 2061 (11th Cir. 1997), *reh'g denied,* 135 F.3d 1409 (11th Cir.), *cert. denied,* 525 U.S. 816, 19S.Ct. 54, 142 L.Ed.2d 42 (1998)

Other
Interpretive Bulletin 75-8, 29 C.F.R. §2509.75-8 (FR-17Q); Interpretive Bulletin 94-2, 29 C.F.R. §2509.94-2(1); DOL Prohibited Transaction Exemption 75-1, Interim Exemption, 40 Fed. Reg. 5201 (Feb. 4, 1975); DOL Information Letter, Prescott Asset Management (1/17/92) (fn. 1); DOL Information Letter, Refco, Inc. (2/13/89); ERISA Technical Release 86-1 (May 22, 1986)

Uniform Prudent Investor Act [UPIA]

§2(a); §2(d); §7; §9(a)

Uniform Prudent Management of Institutional Funds Act [UPMIFA]

§3(b); §3(c); §5(a)

Management of Public Employee Retirement Systems Act [MPERS]

§6(2) and (3); §7(5); §8(a)(3)

FEES FOR INVESTMENT MANAGEMENT ARE CONSISTENT WITH AGREEMENTS AND WITH ALL APPLICABLE LAWS.

The Investment Steward's responsibility in connection with the payment of fees is to determine: (1) whether the fees can be paid from portfolio assets and (2) whether the fees are reasonable in light of the services provided. Accordingly, the Steward should ensure all forms of compensation are reasonable for the services rendered.

Investment Advisor and Investment Manager fees vary widely depending on the asset class to be managed, the size of the account, and whether the funds are to be managed separately or placed into a commingled or mutual fund.

Substantiation

Employee Retirement Income Security Act of 1974 [ERISA]

§3(14)(B); §404(a)(1)(A), (B) and (D); §406(a)

Regulations
29 C.F.R. §2550.408(b)(2)

Other
Booklet: A Look at 401(k) Plan Fees, U.S. Department of Labor, Pension and Welfare Benefits Administration; DOL Advisory Opinion Letter 2001-01A (1/18/01); DOL Advisory Opinion Letter (7/28/98) 1998 WL 1638072; DOL Advisory Opinion Letter 89-28A (9/25/89) 1989 WL 435076; Interpretive Bulletin 75-8, 29 C.F.R. §2509.75-8 (FR-17Q)

Uniform Prudent Investor Act [UPIA]

§2(a); §7 and Comments; §9 Comments

Uniform Prudent Management of Institutional Funds Act [UPMIFA]

§3(b); §3(c); §5(a)

Management of Public Employee Retirement Systems Act [MPERS]

§7(2) and (5); §7 Comments

CRITERIA

4.4.1 A summary of all parties that have been compensated from portfolio assets has been documented, and the fees have been determined to be reasonable given the level of services rendered.

4.4.2 The fees paid to each party are periodically examined to determine whether the fee is consistent with service agreements.

4.4.3 The fees being paid for various services are periodically evaluated for reasonableness.

"FINDER'S FEES" OR OTHER FORMS OF COMPENSATION THAT MAY HAVE BEEN PAID FOR ASSET PLACEMENT ARE APPROPRIATELY APPLIED, UTILIZED, AND DOCUMENTED.

The Investment Steward has a duty to account for all dollars spent on investment management services, whether those dollars are paid directly from the account or in the form of soft dollars and other fee-sharing arrangements. In addition, the Investment Steward has the responsibility to identify those parties that have been compensated from the fees, and to apply a reasonableness test to the amount of compensation received by any party.

In the case of an all-inclusive fee (sometimes referred to as a "bundled" or "wrap" fee) investment product, the Steward should investigate how the various service vendors associated with each component of the all-inclusive fee are compensated to ensure that no one vendor is receiving unreasonable compensation, and to compare the costs of the same services on an *à la carte* basis.

In the case of defined contribution plans, it is customary to offer investment options that carry fees that often are used to offset the plan's record-keeping and administrative costs. For a plan with few assets, such an arrangement may be beneficial for the participants.

However, as the assets grow, the Investment Steward should periodically determine whether it is more advantageous to pay for record-keeping and administrative costs on an *à la carte* basis and switch to mutual funds that have a lower expense ratio in order to reduce the overall expenses of the investment program.

CRITERIA

4.5.1 All parties compensated from portfolio assets have been identified, along with the amount (or schedule) of their compensation.

4.5.2 Compensation paid from portfolio assets has been determined to be fair and reasonable for the services rendered.

Substantiation

Employee Retirement Income Security Act of 1974 [ERISA]

§404(a)(1)(A) and (B);§406(a)(1); §406(b)(1); §406(b)(3)

Case Law
Brock v. Robbins, 830 F.2d 640, 8 E.B.C. 2489 (7th Cir. 1987)

Other
DOL Advisory Opinion Letter 97-15A; DOL Advisory Opinion Letter 97-16A (5/22/97)

Uniform Prudent Investor Act [UPIA]

§2(a); §7; §7 Comments

Case Law
Matter of Derek W. Bryant, 188 Misc. 2d 462, 729 NYS 2d 309 (6/21/01)

Other
McKinneys EPTL11-2.3(d)

Uniform Prudent Management of Institutional Funds Act [UPMIFA]

§3(b); §3(c)

Management of Public Employee Retirement Systems Act [MPERS]

§6(b)(2) and (3); §7(2) and (5)

PRACTICE S-4.6

THERE IS A PROCESS TO PERIODICALLY REVIEW THE ORGANIZATION'S EFFECTIVENESS IN MEETING ITS FIDUCIARY RESPONSIBILITIES.

CRITERIA

4.6.1 Effectiveness of fiduciary Practices is periodically reviewed in order to foster continued improvement.

4.6.2 Assessments are conducted at planned intervals to determine whether (a) appropriate policies and procedures are in place to address all fiduciary obligations, and (b) such policies and procedures are effectively implemented and maintained, and (c) the IPS is up-to-date.

4.6.3 Assessments are documented, conducted in a manner that ensures objectivity and impartiality, and results are reviewed for reasonableness.

Fiduciary duties are generally presented as distinct obligations substantiated through law and regulation. Many of the duties are accompanied by documentation and review obligations. As a practical matter, a comprehensive framework is needed to ensure that all applicable fiduciary practices are fully and effectively addressed on an ongoing basis. A planned approach to conduct periodic assessments provides such a framework.

Given that internal and external reviews and assessments are well-recognized tools to evaluate risks and ensure the effectiveness of policies and procedures, further weight is added to the need to establish a formal overall review process (as is provided by an assessment program).

Finally, it is important to recognize that the trend in law and regulation is towards greater formality in: (1) policies and procedures and (2) processes that ensure that the policies and procedures are effective.

Substantiation

Employee Retirement Income Security Act of 1974 [ERISA]

§404(a)(1)(B)

Case Law
Chao v. Chacon, Case No. 1:04 CV 35000 (N.D. Ohio 2005); *Fink v. National Savings & Trust Co.,* 772 F.2d 951, 957 (D.C. Cir. 1985); *Liss v. Smith,* 991 F.Supp. 278, 299-300 (S.D.N.Y.,1998).

Other
Department of Labor Employee Benefits Security Administration, "Meeting Your Fiduciary Responsibilities" (May 2004); 29 C.F.R. 2509.75-8; 29 C.F.R. 2509.94-2.

Uniform Prudent Investor Act [UPIA]

§2(a); §2(d)

Uniform Management of Public Employee Retirement Systems Act [MPERS]

§8(b); §7

CONCLUSION

The Practices identified in this handbook prescribe a timeless and flexible process for the successful management of investment decisions. Once familiar with the Practices, the Investment Steward will understand that no new investment product or technique is good or bad per se; nor will it be valuable simply because it worked for other fiduciaries. Furthermore, the Practices will help the Steward understand which new investment strategies, products, and techniques fit into their priorities, and which do not.

The intelligent and prudent management of investment decisions requires the Investment Steward to maintain a rational, disciplined investment program. The mind-boggling array of investment choices coupled with market noise from stock markets around the world understandably can result in financial paralysis from information overload. Stewards clearly need a framework for managing investment decisions that allows them to consider developing investment trends, and to thoughtfully navigate the possibilities.

The Board of Directors for the Foundation for Fiduciary Studies

The Staff of Fiduciary360

The AICPA's Personal Financial Planning Executive Committee

APPENDIX A

SAMPLE FIDUCIARY ACKNOWLEDGMENT LETTER

(Date)

(Address of Fiduciary)

Subject: Appointment to Investment Committee

Dear (Fiduciary):

You are hereby appointed to serve as a member of the Investment Committee. As you will be serving as a fiduciary with specific duties and responsibilities which are outlined in the attached handbook [memo], please become familiar with the contents and inform me of any questions and/or concerns you may have regarding your role.

In order to be a successful member of the Investment Committee, you should note the following.

> It does not require extensive experience in securities analysis or portfolio management, but it does require a personal interest in understanding the basics of capital markets.

> It requires a sincere commitment to develop a consensus formulation of goals and objectives with your fellow committee members; the discipline to develop and follow long-term investment policies; the patience to evaluate events calmly in the context of long-term trends; and an understanding of personal and organizational strengths and weaknesses to determine when delegation and outsourcing is more appropriate.

> Most importantly, it requires the ability to get the right things done, otherwise known as effective management. A prudent investment process facilitates effective management by distinguishing important from unimportant tasks.

Please acknowledge receipt of this letter and your understanding of your fiduciary duties and responsibilities by signing and returning the attached Acceptance Letter to me.

Sincerely,

(Plan Sponsor, Trustee, or Settlor)

Enclosure: *Prudent Practices for Investment Stewards* handbook (or comparable memo)

Sample Fiduciary Acceptance Letter

Date: (Date)

To: (Plan Sponsor, Trustee, or Settlor)

From: (Fiduciary)

Subject: **Appointment to Investment Committee**

I hereby accept my appointment to serve as a member of the Investment Committee. I understand the fiduciary duties and responsibilities associated with my appointment.

Sincerely,

(Fiduciary)

APPENDIX B

SAMPLE INVESTMENT COMMITTEE MEETING MINUTES

Date: _____   Time: _____

_____ Regularly scheduled   _____ Special

Attendees (list):   Was there a quorum (circle)? Yes/No

Matters Discussed:

Materials Reviewed:

Decisions voted upon:

SAMPLE BY-LAWS AND OPERATING PROCEDURES FOR THE INVESTMENT COMMITTEE

Section 1: Formation of the Investment Committee

1.1 Functions of the Committee

The Investment Committee (Committee) shall perform the functions of an investment fiduciary responsible for the prudent management of the Investment Portfolio (Portfolio). The Committee will comply with all applicable fiduciary, prudence, and due diligence requirements experienced investment professionals would utilize; and with all applicable laws, rules, and regulations that may impact the Portfolio. The Committee shall have the exclusive authority to establish, execute and interpret an investment policy statement for the Portfolio. The Committee shall be responsible for the selection and retention of professional advisors to the Portfolio, which may include, but not necessarily be limited to, Investment Managers, an Investment Advisor, custodians, attorneys, accountants, and clerical staff.

1.2 Definition of a Fiduciary

A fiduciary is defined as a person who has the legal and/or implied moral responsibility to manage the assets of another person. A fiduciary must act solely in the best interests of that person. The Committee is subject to certain duties and responsibilities, including, but not limited to:

1. Know the standards, laws, and trust provisions that impact the investment process of the Portfolio

2. Prudently diversify the Portfolio to a specific risk/return profile (Or in the case of a participant-directed retirement plan, to make sufficient asset classes available so that a participant can prudently diversify his or her portfolio)

3. Prepare, execute, and maintain an investment policy statement

4. Have investment decisions made by prudent experts

5. Control and account for all investment-related expenses

6. Monitor the activities of all investment-related service vendors

7. Avoid conflicts of interest and prohibited transactions

1.3 Establishment of Committee

The Committee shall consist of such number of individuals as are appointed by the Sponsor. Any member of the Committee may resign, and his or her successor, if any, shall be appointed by the Chairman. Each Committee member will acknowledge the acceptance of appointment to the Committee in writing. No Committee member shall have the authority to bind the Committee in any contract or endeavor without the expressed written authority of the majority of the Committee members.

1.4 Establishment of Officers

The Committee shall have an office of Chairman and a Secretary. The Chairman shall be responsible for the conduct of all the meetings of the Committee and shall have voting rights the same as any other Committee member. The Chairman shall perform such other duties as the Committee may assign, and shall be the designated Agent for service of legal process.

The Secretary shall be responsible for keeping minutes of the transactions of the Committee and shall be the official custodian of records of the Committee. The Secretary, together with the Chairman, shall execute all official contracts of the Committee. The Secretary shall compile Committee agendas. The Chairman and Secretary are authorized by the Committee to execute any instruments necessary for the Committee to conduct business.

APPENDIX C

SAMPLE BY-LAWS AND OPERATING PROCEDURES FOR THE INVESTMENT COMMITTEE

1.5 Disclosure and Conflict of Interest

Notwithstanding any provision of law, no Committee member shall vote or participate in a determination of any matter in which the Committee member shall receive a special private gain. Committee members have a duty of loyalty that precludes them from being influenced by motives other than the accomplishment of the purposes of the Portfolio. Committee members, in the performance of their duties, must conform and act pursuant to the documents and instruments establishing and governing the Portfolio.

Section II: Meetings

2.1 Attendance at Board Meetings

The Committee shall set its own schedule of meetings. Special meetings may be called by the Chairman or by a majority of the Committee members. The Committee shall meet at least once each quarter. Notices of meetings shall not be required if waived by all members of the Committee. In recognition of the importance of the work of the Committee, regular attendance at the Committee meetings is expected from all members. Any member who fails to attend two consecutive meetings of the Committee without an excuse acceptable to the other Committee members shall be deemed to have resigned from the Committee. A majority of the members of the Committee at the time in office shall constitute a quorum for the transaction of business. The action of the Committee shall be determined by the vote or other affirmative expression by the majority of its members in attendance where a quorum is present.

2.2 Agendas and Other Meeting Materials

An agenda shall be prepared for each regular and special meeting of the Committee. The agenda shall set forth those items upon which the Committee anticipates taking action or discussing. Each agenda item shall have attached backup material necessary for discussion or action by the Committee. A copy of the agenda and backup material shall be furnished to each Committee member prior to commencement of the meeting. Full and complete minutes detailing records of deliberations and decisions shall be maintained and held by the Secretary. The Secretary shall record all acts and determinations of the Committee, and all such records shall be preserved in the custody of the Secretary. Such record and documents shall be open at all times for inspection by Committee members or for the purpose of making copies by any person designated by the Sponsor.

2.3 Rules of Order

In recognition of the importance of accomplishing the objectives of the Committee in a most orderly fashion, the Committee may establish rules of order or bylaws for the conduct of its meetings.

2.4 Appearance before the Committee

All persons who are scheduled to make appearances before the Committee shall be scheduled through the Secretary, and the Committee may establish the time limits established for such meetings. Appearances before the Committee may be in person or through a representative. All communications with the Committee shall either be in writing to the Secretary, teleconference, or by personal appearance at a Committee meeting.

_____

Chairman

GLOSSARY OF TERMS

This glossary was compiled from the following sources:

> Eugene B. Burroughs, CFA, *Investment Terminology* (Revised Edition), International Foundation of Employee Benefit Plans, Inc., 1993.
>
> John Downes and Jordan Elliot Goodman, *Dictionary of Finance and Investment Terms* (Third Edition), Barron's Educational Series, Inc., 1991.
>
> John W. Guy, *How to Invest Someone Else's Money*, Irwin Professional Publishing, Burr Ridge, Illinois, 1994.
>
> Donald B. Trone, William R. Allbright, and Philip R. Taylor, *The Management of Investment Decisions*, Irwin Professional Publishing, Burr Ridge, Illinois, 1995.
>
> Donald B. Trone, William R. Allbright, and Philip R. Taylor, *Procedural Prudence for Fiduciaries*, self-published, 1997.

Alpha – This statistic measures a portfolio's return in excess of the market return adjusted for risk. It is a measure of the Manager's contribution to performance with reference to security selection. A positive alpha indicates that a portfolio was positively rewarded for the residual risk, which was taken for that level of market exposure.

Analyst – A person approved by CEFEX or fi360 to conduct an assessment for *Certification*.

Assessment – The process of determining whether a fiduciary conforms with defined *Practices* and *Criteria*.

Asset Allocation – The process of determining the optimal allocation of a fund's portfolio among broad asset classes.

Audit – (*verb*) The process of gathering, displaying, and verifying information and data that will be used to assess whether there is conformance with a *Standard*:

Basis Point – One hundredth of a percent (100 Basis Points = 1%).

Best Execution – Formally defined as the difference between the execution price (the price at which a security is actually bought or sold) and the "fair market price," which involves calculating opportunity costs by examining the security price immediately after the trade is placed. Best execution occurs when the trade involves no lost opportunity cost; for example, when there is no increase in the price of a security shortly after it is sold.

Cash Sweep Accounts – A money market fund into which all new contributions, stock dividend income, and bond interest income is placed ("swept") for a certain period of time. At regular intervals, or when rebalancing is necessary, this cash is invested in assets in line with the asset allocation stipulated in the IPS.

CFA Institute (formerly AIMR) Performance Presentation Standards – These standards, effective January 1, 1993, are designed to promote full disclosure and fair representation in the reporting of investment results in order to provide uniformity in comparing Manager results. These standards include ethical principles, and apply to all organizations serving investment management functions. Compliance is verified at two levels: Level 1 and Level 2. (Level 2 is a more comprehensive verification process).

Commingled Fund – An investment fund that is similar to a mutual fund in that investors purchase and redeem units that represent ownership in a pool of securities. Commingled funds usually are offered through a bank-administered plan allowing for broader and more efficient investing.

Commission Recapture – An agreement by which a plan Fiduciary earns credits based upon the amount of brokerage commissions paid. These credits can be used for services that will benefit the plan such as consulting services, custodian fees, or hardware and software expenses.

Correlation Coefficient – Correlation measures the degree to which two variables are associated. Correlation is a commonly used tool for constructing a well-diversified portfolio. Traditionally, equities and fixed-income asset returns have not moved closely together. The asset returns are not strongly correlated. A balanced fund with equities and fixed-income assets represents a diversified portfolio that attempts to take advantage of the low correlation between the two asset classes.

Criteria – The details of a defined *Practice* and serve as the basis for a Global Standard of Excellence.

Directed Brokerage – Circumstances in which a board of trustees or other fiduciary requests that the Investment Manager direct trades to a particular broker so that the commissions generated can be used for specific services \or resources. See "**Soft Dollars.**"

Economically-Targeted Investment (**ETI**) – Investments where the goal is to target a certain economic activity, sector, or area in order to produce corollary benefits in addition to the main objective of earning a competitive risk-adjusted rate of return.

ERISA – The Employee Retirement Income Security Act is a 1974 U.S. law governing the operation of most private pension and benefit plans. The law eased pension eligibility rules, set up the Pension Benefit Guaranty Corporation, and established guidelines for the management of pension funds.

Fiduciary – From the Latin word *fiducia*, meaning "trust." Someone who stands in a special relation of trust, confidence, and/or legal responsibility. A fiduciary is held to a standard of conduct and trust above that of a stranger or of a casual business person due to the superior knowledge and/or training of the fiduciary.

Fiduciary Adviser – A term introduced under the 2006 Pension Protection Act; an Investment Advisor selected by an ERISA plan sponsor to provide specific investment advice to plan participants.

Fiduciary Excellence – Is a function of how well *Investment Stewards, Investment Advisors,* and *Investment Managers* follow defined fiduciary *Practices* and *Criteria.*

Investment Advisor – A professional fiduciary who is responsible for managing comprehensive and continuous investment decisions (including wealth managers, financial advisors, trust officers, financial consultants, investment consultants, and financial planners).

Investment Manager – A professionals who has discretion to select specific securities for separate accounts, mutual funds, commingled trusts, and unit trusts.

Investment Steward – A person who has the legal responsibility for managing investment decisions (trustees and investment committee members).

Liquidity Risk – The risk that there will be insufficient cash to meet the fund's disbursement and expense requirements.

Money Markets – Financial markets in which financial assets with a maturity of less than one year are traded. Money market funds also refer to open-end mutual funds that invest in low-risk, highly liquid, short-term financial instruments and whose net asset value is kept stable at $1 per share. The average portfolio maturity is 30 to 60 days.

Practice – (*noun*) The details of a prudent process.

Proxy Voting – A written authorization given by a shareholder to someone else to vote his or her shares at a stockholders annual or special meeting called to elect directors or for some other corporate purpose.

Rater – A person approved by CEFEX to conduct a *Rating*.

Rating – The process of determining whether a fiduciary exceeds, and to what degree it exceeds, a *Standard*.

Real Estate Investment Trust (REIT) – An investment fund whose objective is to hold real estate-related assets; either through mortgages, construction and development loans, or equity interests.

Risk-Adjusted Return – The return on an asset, or portfolio, modified to explicitly account for the risk of the asset or portfolio.

Risk-Free Rate of Return – The return on 90-day U.S. Treasury Bills. This is used as a proxy for no risk due to its zero default risk issuance, minimal "interest rate" risk and high marketability. The term is really a misnomer since nothing is free of risk. It is utilized since certain economic models require a "risk-free" point of departure. See **Sharpe Ratio**.

R-squared (R^2 or R2) – Formally called the coefficient of determination, this measures the overall strength or "explanatory power" of a statistical relationship. In general, a higher R2 means a stronger statistical relationship between the variables that have been estimated, and therefore more confidence in using the estimation for decision-making. Primarily used to determine the appropriateness of a given index in evaluating a Manager's performance.

Safe Harbor Rules – A series of guidelines which, when in full compliance, may limit a fiduciary's liabilities.

Sharpe Ratio – This statistic is a commonly used measure of risk-adjusted return. It is calculated by subtracting the Risk-Free Return (usually 3-Month U.S. Treasury Bill) from the portfolio return and dividing the resulting "excess return" by the portfolio's total risk level (standard deviation). The result is a measure of return gained per unit of total risk taken. The Sharpe Ratio can be used to compare the relative performance of Managers. If two managers have the same level of risk but different levels of excess return, the manager with the higher Sharpe Ratio would be preferable. The Sharpe Ratio is most helpful when comparing managers with both different returns and different levels of risk. In this case, the Sharpe Ratio provides a per-unit measure of the two managers that enables a comparison.

Socially-Targeted Investment or Socially Responsible Investment (SRI) – An investment that is undertaken based upon social, rather than purely financial, guidelines. See also **Economically-Targeted Investment**.

Soft Dollars – The portion of a commission's expense for trading a security which is in excess of the actual cost of executing the trade by the broker-dealer.

Standard of Excellence – The *Practices* and *Criteria* which detail a prudent process and the attributes of a trustworthy fiduciary.

Components of a Standard

Standard Deviation – A statistical measure of portfolio risk. It reflects the average deviation of the observations from their sample mean. Standard deviation is used as an estimate of risk since it measures how wide the range of returns typically is. The wider the typical range of returns, the higher the standard deviation of returns, and the higher the portfolio risk. If returns were normally distributed (i.e., has a bell-shaped curve distribution) then approximately two-thirds of the returns would occur within plus or minus one standard deviation from the sample mean.

Strategic Asset Allocation – Rebalancing back to the normal mix at specified time intervals (quarterly) or when established tolerance bands are violated (±5%).

Tactical Asset Allocation – The "first cousin" to **Market Timing** because it uses certain "indicators" to make adjustments in the proportions of portfolio invested in three asset classes – stocks, bonds, and cash.

Trading Costs – Behind investment management fees, trading accounts for the second highest cost of plan administration. Trading costs are usually quoted in cents per share. As of the date of this publication, median institutional trading costs range from 5 to 7 cents per share.

90-Day U.S. Treasury Bill – The 90-Day T-Bill provides a measure of riskless return. The rate of return is the average interest rate available in the beginning of each month for a T-Bill maturing in 90 days. In Europe, the London Inter-Bank Offered Rate (LIBOR) is also used as a risk-free benchmark.

Variance – A statistical measure that indicates the spread of values within a set of outcomes around a calculated average. For example, the range of daily prices for a stock will have a variance over a time period that reflects the amount that the stock price varies from the average, or mean, price of the stock over the time period. Variance is useful as a risk statistic because it gives an indication of how much the value of the portfolio might fluctuate up or down from the average value over a given time.